Mining for Gold:

Climbing Mount Empathy

and

Reclaiming the Mystical

by Charles C. Finn

Cover photo:

Carpeting a beech forest in Belgium
are wild hyacinth bluebells
called into color by the rising sun.

Dedication

"I familiarized myself with writers across centuries who would in time become as closely related to me as my personal friends." (Howard Thurman)

With several exceptions
most of those quoted in the following pages
I have never met.
Irrelevant it feels
as they, too, have become true friends.
To them all this small book is dedicated.

Table of Contents

Part One: Climbing Mount Empathy

Part Two: Reclaiming the Mystical

Part One:

Climbing Mount Empathy

Foreword to *Climbing Mount Empathy*

I have this thing for words, especially those containing secret fire, like empathy. Empathy seems a mild word, warm perhaps but hardly fiery. Webster's definition of empathy as "the imaginative projection of a subjective state into an object so that the object appears to be infused with it" hardly suggests ardor.

Over the years I have had an eye out for writers who do empathy more justice, help us *feel* its fire, or, changing the metaphor, help us recognize the challenge and achievement of climbing the imposing mountain of it. Come listen to these reflections on the force and the depth and the reach of this blazing, mountainous word we call empathy.

Loren Eiseley

A more eloquent expression of praise for empathy could scarcely be found than this from the nature-essayist, Loren Eiseley. He might have entitled the following "In Defense of Stepping Over a Cricket." "No, it is not because I am filled with obscure guilt that I step gently over, and not upon, an autumn cricket. I possess empathy; I have grown with man in his mind's growing. I share that sympathy and compassion which extends beyond the barriers of class and race and form until it partakes of the universal whole...The most enormous extension of vision of which life is capable: the projection of itself into other lives."

Eiseley's simple statement that he possesses empathy was not a boast. A student of evolution's stupendously long march through time, Eiseley was simply acknowledging the innate capacity of the human mind *to grow* and his astonishment in his own participation in this growth. He helps us appreciate anew words we take for granted, sympathy and compassion, highlighting that, connected as they are to our capacity for empathy, these in fact constitute extraordinary evolutionary breakthroughs. Think of it: "the most enormous extension of vision of which life is capable: the projection of itself into other lives."

Howard Thurman

Empathy, unnamed, radiates from this passage from Howard Thurman's *The Luminous Darkness.*"The place where the imagination shows its greatest power as the agent of God is in the miracle which it creates when one man, standing where he is, is able to put himself in another man's place...to establish a beachhead in another man's spirit...I suddenly imagined I was a Jew...I reshaped my address with that imaginative leap."

We don't usually think of imagination as a power--a flight, perhaps, a leap into possibility--but here this prophet-theologian sees its greatest power, as the agent of God no less, *for creating miracles*. How more forcefully could he describe the wonder of being able to imagine oneself into another life that ensues "when one man, standing where he is, is able to put himself in another man's place...to establish a beachhead in another man's spirit."

The context for Thurman's remarks was when he learned that the audience for a talk he had prepared was Jewish. By imagining himself a Jew, thus establishing a kind of beachhead in their spirit, he was able to reshape his words to fit, so to speak, their ears. We normally might think of this as a skill every effective speaker or entertainer employs in order to better reach an audience. But by calling it a miracle Thurman jolts us into a recognition of how extraordinary a feat this is. The fact that this kind of empathy comes so naturally to some makes it, in Howard Thurman's eyes, no less a miracle.

Henry David Thoreau

"I cannot but see still in my mind's eye those little striped breams poised in Walden's glaucous water...I can only poise my thought there by its side and try to think like a bream for a moment. I can only think of precious jewels, of music, poetry, beauty, and the mystery of life. I only see the bream in its orbit, as I see a star...The bream, appreciated, floats in the pond as the centre of the system, another image of God. Its life no man can explain more than he can his own. I want you to perceive the mystery of the bream... Acquaintance with it is to make my life more rich and eventful." (Thoreau's *Journal*)

First there was Thoreau's close observation, not just of small fish but of "little striped breams," not just swimming but "poised," not just in Walden Pond but "in Walden's glaucous water."

He is then curious enough about this small fish to try not just to understand it but *to enter into it,* or rather to e*nter into it in order to understand it*: "I can only poise my thought there by its side and try to think like a bream for a moment."

Why in the world would he even try to "poise" his thought there by its side, to "think like a bream" even for a second, were he not convinced there was consciousness here? What respect to accord a life lower than the human, intuiting that it, too, possesses a mind of its own! Before curiosity had to come an elemental caring.

The wonder of what he sees calls the poet out of Thoreau, metaphor rolling after metaphor. "I can only think of precious jewels, of music, poetry, beauty, and the mystery of life. I only see the bream in its orbit, as I see a star." From the infinitesimal to the infinite in a flash. Where can the mystical wings of imagination not carry us?

Then the key word, *appreciated*, followed by a quintessentially Transcendendalist declaration: "The bream, appreciated, floats in the pond as the centre of the system, another image of God." There is absolutely nothing, Thoreau is asserting, that does not swim like a fish in the mystery of God. We are far beyond reason's reach here. "Its life no man can explain more than he can his own."

"I want you to perceive the mystery of the bream." The sudden "you" reveals Thoreau's anticipation of an eventual wider audience. Coming upon amazing good news that has enriched his life, his fervent hope is to pass it on. Nowhere in these journal entries that we have been considering has Thoreau used the actual word "empathy," but does not this whole passage sing of it? Webster's prose statement: "empathy: the imaginative projection of a subjective state into an object so that the object appears to be infused with it." Thoreau's poetic flight: "Think like a bream for a moment."

Carl Rogers

As staunch a champion of empathy as was the psychologist Carl Rogers, he insisted the place to begin to understand its power and reach is to grasp the foundation it stands upon, which he termed "unconditional positive regard." Here is how he put it: "It is impossible to accurately sense the perceptual world of another person unless you value that person—unless you care." If I do not regard you as having value as a unique-in-all-the-world human being, if I do not care about you in this elemental sense, then I am not going to make the effort to imagine myself into your unique-in-all-the-world perspective on things when you speak. Rogers is not saying you must *like* the person speaking any more than that you must *agree* with what she or he is saying. What he is saying is that you will never come to understand the "felt meaning" behind the words spoken, much less then be able to communicate accurately what you have heard, without *caring enough to listen.* "An empathic therapist points sensitively to the 'felt meaning' which the client is experiencing in this particular moment."

Of all the schools of psychotherapy, Rogers' person-centered approach is likely the most easily dismissed for seeming to counsel little beyond reflecting back ("parroting" according to his critics) to the client what has been heard, as if that would engender some kind of transformation. Rogers would not disagree that the aim of his approach is transformation (he preferred to call it self-actualization), but he would simply insist that if transformation is ever to happen, empathy is the *sine qua non.* "A high degree of empathy is possibly *the* most potent factor in bringing about change and learning." He goes on, countering the dismissive view that empathy is both simple and easy : "Being empathic is a complex, demanding, and strong—yet also a subtle and gentle—way of being." He is clearly not just talking about another tool in the counselor's toolbox here, rather something so far deeper he can only call it "a way of being." "Parroting" doesn't come close to the "vast complex process" of listening and reflecting that is required.

We can gain a glimpse into the vastness and complexity of this process, and perhaps begin to come to an appreciation of the mountain empathy invites us to climb, when seeing what Rogers boiled it down to when counseling those in conflict: "Articulate the other's view as well as he does himself so that he knows you have heard him." This will sound simple to any who has not tried it. The achievement, first of deep listening, then of careful articulation of the felt meaning behind the words heard, is less an amble up a hill than a scaling of an Everest.

William Shakespeare

How might someone armed with empathy have responded back in Shakespeare's day to the plight of the homeless? We need look no further than a blinded old fool of a king wandering piteously in a storm at night, suddenly, scales falling from his eyes, brought to his senses.

"Poor naked wretches, wheresoe'er you are,/ That bide the pelting of this pitiless storm,/ How shall your houseless heads and unfed sides,/ Your looped and windowed raggedness, defend you/ From seasons such as these? O, I have ta'en/ Too little care of this! Take physic, pomp;/ Expose thyself to feel what wretches feel,/ That thou mayst shake the superflux to them/ And show the heavens more just."

"Expose thyself to feel what wretches feel"--How better capture empathy's arduous challenge? It took catastrophe to bring King Lear to his knees, folly and blindness to finally open his inner eye, but what redemption he finally found! Empathy comes to some easy, but to many it may take a near total undoing before any thought of showing the heavens more just by shaking the superflux to those most in need of it.

Brian Swimme

"Our human imagination brought something radically new to Earth's life: the capacity to experience the world from another's perspective. We call this empathy."

There are several wonders here on which the cosmic storyteller Brian Swimme shines a spotlight. The first is the link between empathy and the human imagination. What is empathy, Swimme points out, but an imagining into the world of another that human beings alone in all the known universe are capable of? For every shrine to Memory, for holding in consciousness things that have been, let there be a shrine to Imagination for opening up windows of possibility to things that *may be*. We remember and we dream--how awesome is that?

But Swimme also calls our attention to how radically new this capacity to dream ourselves into other worlds is. Against the long backdrop of evolutionary history, Earth finally emerges, but then how much longer till the birth on Earth of *life*, and then eons more until the birth of *consciousness*, and still eons more until the stunning emergence of a *self-consciousness* that can imagine itself beyond the confines of its own self-interest and self-preservation. A truly awesome thing is imagination, and its prodigious child empathy.

Implied in Swimme's quotation is the wonder of perspective, the stepping back to see the big picture, the ability to put things in context, the capacity to imagine ourselves into another's world which widens our own world in the process. Imagination, empathy, perspective--a cosmic storyteller here interweaves all three.

Frederick Buechner and May Sarton

Empathy calls to mind passages from two writers I have long admired, Frederick Buechner and May Sarton, who pondered the worlds behind human faces. While neither used the word empathy in the passages that follow, their musings make manifest its presence.

First from Frederick Buechner : "Faces like everything else can be looked at and not seen." Buechner goes on to reveal where it took him one day, looking long enough at human faces until he began to see. "The odds are that for at least one other person somewhere in the world each of them—even the unlikeliest—matters enormously, or mattered enormously once, or someday, with any luck, will come to matter." Take up Buechner's implicit invitation. Look at the next human face that your glance takes in, and realize that this human being *matters enormously to some-one*--past, present, or possibly future. Suddenly this face takes on gigantic proportions, opens a great mystery. To *someone*, this face, and the long history and mystery of the story behind it, matters, enormously! Perhaps every bush is burning, before which (if we could but see it) we would take off our shoes. Is that not where these words of Frederick Buechner take us if empathy shows the way?

And then there's May Sarton's glowing phrase--"that great miracle, a human face"--that shakes awake our vision. Can anything in the universe quite compare with the revelation etched in the face of an individual human being, manifestation both of a personal history and the history of the cosmos? Love, she goes on to declare, in league with empathy we might add, "is one of the great enlargers of the person because it requires us to 'take in' the stranger and to understand him." The greater the empathy, the larger the person--what spirit impoverishment without it!

Hermann Hesse and Black Elk

Back in the late 60s and early 70s I devoured everything I could get my hands on by Hermann Hesse, holding a special place in my heart for his *Wandering*. Perhaps his simplest book, in it he dreams himself into a variety of people he spies from a distance or encounters up close. Here is a passage in which Hesse captures the essence of empathy, championing its reach without using the word. "I want my soul to be a wandering thing, able to move back into a hundred forms. I want to dream myself into priests and wanderers, female cooks and murderers, children and animals, and, more than anything else, birds and trees. That is necessary."

Native Americans would resonate deeply with this, as the wanderer dreams himself not only into every manner of human being, lofty or lowly, but more than anything else into animals and birds and trees. When the Sioux end all their rituals with "*mitakuye oyasin!*" (all our relations), they have in mind far more than simply the two-leggeds. As Black Elk put it, "Is not the sky a father and the earth a mother, and are not all living things with feet or wings or roots their children?...All things are the works of the Great Spirit. We should know that He is within all things: the trees, the grasses, the rivers, the mountains, and all the four-legged animals, and the winged peoples...With all beings and all things we shall be as relatives." No world is barred to the wandering imagination or to its extension we call empathy.

Vernon Ruland

My high school English teacher, Vernon Ruland, subsequently became to me both mentor and friend. To say that he esteemed empathy highly is to understate. In his memoir, *Living Out the Questions: A Jesuit Confession*, he comes at empathy from multiple angles. The first highlights its uneven distribution among humans. "Some people find no trace of empathy in their bones. But others seem to have entered life with a temperament and imagination almost preternaturally empathic."

But, ironically, what can help educate one in empathy, he learned, are difficult life circumstances. "Perhaps from my own ordeal as an introverted adolescent I felt empathy for any person unable to fit in, especially the potential scapegoat." And then again, "Just next door to failure myself, I feel empathy now for underdogs." Before pitying one abused, he is reminding us, let us remember where such an ordeal can lead, whom it can heal. And on this subject of healing, "Empathy has the power to heal both the person feeling it and the person toward whom it is felt."

While clearly emulating empathy, Ruland added an important qualification. "Empathy has its boundaries. My own sufferings are uniquely my own...I can never understand fully how anyone else's burden feels inside." May this be a cautionary reminder before we think of assuring another, "I know exactly how you feel."

Ruland acknowledged that he himself possessed empathy, in fact felt it was not unrelated to his calling to be a priest. "What qualifies me to be a priest, I am convinced, is mostly my human empathy...[my ability] to feel for others when they are ignorant and make mistakes."

Lame Deer and James Baldwin

The following from *Lame Deer, Seeker of Visions* will be an empathy mountain to climb, especially if you are American and your skin is white:

"What does this Mount Rushmore mean to us Indians? It means that these big white faces are telling us, 'First we gave you Indians a treaty that you could keep these Black Hills forever, as long as the sun would shine, in exchange for all the Dakotas, Wyoming and Montana. Then we found the gold and took that last piece of land, because we were stronger, and there were more of us than there were of you, and because we had cannons and Gatling guns, while you hadn't even progressed far enough to make a steel knife. And when you didn't want to leave, we wiped you out, and those of you who survived we put on reservations. And then we took the gold out, a billion bucks, and we aren't through yet. And because we like the tourist dollars, too, we have made your sacred Black Hills into one vast Disneyland. And after we did all this we carved up this mountain, the dwelling place of your spirits, and put our four gleaming white faces here. We are the conquerors.' They could just as well have carved this mountain into a huge cavalry boot standing on a dead Indian."

The following from James Baldwin's *The Fire Next Time* will be another empathy mountain to climb, especially if you are American and your skin is white:

"You must put yourself in the skin of a man who is wearing the uniform of his country, is a candidate for death in its defense, and who is called a "nigger" by his comrades-in-arms and his officers; who is almost always given the hardest, ugliest, most menial work to do...and who watches German prisoners of war treated by Americans with more human dignity than he has ever received at their hands. And who, at the same time, as a human being, is far freer in a strange land than he has ever been at home. *Home!* The very word begins to have a despairing and diabolical ring...Search, in his shoes, for a job, for a place to live; ride, in his skin, on segregated buses; see, with his eyes, the signs saying 'White' and 'Colored,' and especially the signs that say 'White Ladies' and 'Colored *Women*'; look into the eyes of his wife; look into the eyes of his son; listen, with his ears, to political speeches, North and South; imagine yourself being told to 'wait.'"

Prose and Poetry to End With

Here are two final things to ponder relating to the vital importance of empathy in our lives, one in prose by the author Julius Lester accenting the cost, one in a poem of my own accenting the gain.

"History is not just facts and events. History is also a pain in the heart, and we repeat history until we are able to make another's pain in the heart our own."

Putting it into Overdrive

It's surprising how fast they move.
When you think caterpillar you think slow,
but woolly ones trying to cross the road
put it into overdrive.
Still it takes at least a minute
with every passing car wheel threatening squash.
At a relaxed speed on a country road,
if you've a mind to be on the lookout,
you can spot them at enough distance
to veer slightly and avert squashing.
I have to believe they appreciate
the chance to keep on trucking.

Afterword

The foregoing passages paying tribute to the explosive significance of empathy are of course not exhaustive. The author, in fact, invites any of his readers who run across other testimonies to empathy to pass them along to him. If he is ever led to expand on the fire of empathy's mountain, he will then have more riches to draw upon.

Charles C. Finn
October 2019

Part Two:

Reclaiming the Mystical

Foreword to *Reclaiming the Mystical*

Words lure sometimes, especially those that not only defy exact definition but are dismissed by many for precisely that reason--"too vague, too murky." Mystical, mystic and mysticism are such words. The thrust of the pages that follow is that there are immense things that these words point to, treasures, if you will, waiting to be mined. Listen first of all to an esteemed representative of the scientific community, Albert Einstein.

"The most beautiful emotion we can experience is the mystical. It is the power of all true art and science. He to whom this emotion is a stranger, who can no longer wonder, stand rapt in awe, is as good as dead."

The first intriguing thing here: Einstein labels the mystical an *emotion*, and the most beautiful one at that. And then he refers to it not only as a *power* but as the power "*of all true art and science.*" Let those words sink in. Finally, before ending with a lament for those who are strangers to this most powerful and beautiful of human emotions, he highlights wonder and standing "rapt in awe" as its most striking feature.

Next listen to an esteemed representative of the religious community, Karl Rahner, a Jesuit priest who is widely regarded as one of the most influential Catholic theologians of the 20th century whose writings played an enormous role in shaping the documents of the Second Vatican Council. Rahner famously observed that Christians of the future will be mystics or there will be no Christianity. And elsewhere, "In the days ahead, you will either be a mystic, one who has experienced God for real, or nothing at all." Rahner gives here only one clue as to what he believes constitutes a mystic, but it is a vast one: "one who has experienced God for real."

If towering wisdom figures in the worlds of science and religion have in common the highest regard for the mystical, we might be prompted to mine for its gold. Come read a host of others, no less enamored of things mystical than Einstein and Rahner, who invite us to start mining.

Carl Rogers

If the quest is to delve deeper into mysticism, searching for its possible relevance to every day, down-to-Earth lives of ordinary people, Carl Rogers would not seem to be one to turn to. After all, was not his arena of concern psychology and counseling rather than religion or mysticism? Let's not be so sure. Here is an older Rogers looking back. "When I am closest to my inner intuitive self, then whatever I do seems to be full of healing. Then simply my *presence* is releasing...At these moments it seems that my inner spirit has reached out and touched the inner spirit of the other...Our relationship has become part of something larger. I realize this account partakes of the mystical. I, like many others, have underestimated the importance of this mystical, spiritual dimension."

While Rogers never pinned down what precisely he meant by "this mystical, spiritual dimension," he had given some clues: intuitive self, healing presence, inner spirits reaching out and touching. Perhaps he came closest with "Our relationship has become part of something larger." How better acknowledge the realm of mystery encompassing us all than by saying it "partakes of the mystical"? Perhaps Carl Rogers is just one more wise one reminding us that when it comes to the mystical, clues are as close as we can come. So let us continue in our search for clues.

Rumi

It is helpful to remember when reading translations of the poetry of Jalal-al-Din Rumi (13th century Persian poet) that he is said never to have written a word of it. Rather, as a member of the Sufi "whirling dervish" branch of the Muslim faith, Rumi would go into ecstatic trances for hours, uttering things that his devoted disciples would then write down and pass on to others, extending now more than seven centuries! It should not come as a surprise that Rumi had some hints into mysticism to share with the world.

"Tree limbs rise and fall like the ecstatic arms of those who have submitted to the mystical life." Or elsewhere, "The wind is the Holy Spirit. The trees are Mary." To Rumi the mystic's key is the very meaning of Islam: submission.

"Let mystics constantly remember...kindle remembering in others." Shifting the key to remembrance. Rumi leads us to wonder, Just what is it mystics are constantly to remember, and why such passion to kindle it in others?

"Mystics are experts in laziness. They rely on it, because they continuously see God working all around them. The harvest keeps coming in, yet they never even did the plowing." If we think of the harvests we keep receiving, thanks to no effort of our own--air for breathing, sun for warmth, rain for nourishment--how then not bask in endless humility and gratitude?

"Your deepest need and desire is satisfied by the moment's energy here in your hand"--is this not reminiscent of a Jewish mystic twenty centuries ago who kept intoning, "The kingdom of heaven is at hand"? Here at hand, right where we stand--can they be serious?

"The mystic flies from moment to moment." The hummingbird comes to mind, flying from one flower to another. Hummingbird Rumi invites us, too, to keep flying without ever once leaving home.

Matthew Fox

Matthew Fox, an Episcopal (formerly Catholic) priest, ever sings in his many books of a living cosmology which is composed of three essential ingredients: "The holy trinity of science (knowledge of creation), mysticism (experiential union with creation and its unnamable mysteries), and art (expression of our awe at creation) is what constitute a living cosmology."

It is noteworthy, regarding mysticism, that it is not just union that Fox underscores but *experiential* union, less an intellectual assent that the cosmos literally is a "uni-verse," than a grounded personal *experience* of the grand communion of all that is. Too, rather than saying that this is a union with the transcendental source of all that is, he states that it is experienced "with creation and its unnamable mysteries." No separation is implied between supernatural and natural, Creator and creation--hence the emphasis on a "creation spirituality" that is the domain of scientist as well as mystic.

"Mystic and scientist alike are urging humanity to a new level of consciousness, a new awareness of the interdependence of all things...By emphasizing that the Spirit of God dwells in us all, creation spirituality liberates the mystic in us all...Mystics believe there is a conspiracy in the universe on their behalf." Another way Fox might have put this is if you have not yet come to discover the joyous conspiracy of the universe acting on your behalf, then you have likely not yet fully realized your own inner mystic. Once *experiencing* that you are a living participant in the Grand Communion, you are liberated from your likely prior assumption of separation, if not alienation, from the very heart of the universe.

Fox here is sounding a note that goes against the grain of the common presumption that mystics are at a far remove from ordinary people struggling with the nitty-gritty of everyday life. Fox instead is insisting that there is within each and every one of us a mystic awaiting liberation, awaiting the realization that the Source of it all dwells in us as in every other member of the living body of the cosmos!

And where does the awe of creation come in, so essential to art's role in what Fox considers the holy trinity of a living cosmology? "Awe is the mystical response to the cosmos...The experience of awe is divinity's way of getting through to us yet another time." So if you believe you must be beyond the reach of a mysticism reserved for the spiritually elite, Fox would agree only if you are incapable of experiencing awe. Put more positively, to the degree that beauty of any kind, human or natural, arrests your attention, catches your breath, or touches your heart, to that degree Fox is asserting the mystic inside of you is alive and well.

And where does a thirst for justice come in? "Healthy religion calls people to be both lovers (mystics) and prophets (warriors defending what one cherishes). Love very much embraces our struggles for justice."

Frederick Buechner

There is a lot to unpack, as the saying goes, in the following quotations on the subject of mysticism from the Presbyterian minister/writer Frederick Buechner.

"Every man is a mystic because every man at one time or another experiences in the thick of his joy or his pain the power out of the depths of his life to bless him. I do not believe that it matters greatly what name you call this power—the Spirit of God is only one of its names—but what I think does matter, vastly, is that we open ourselves to receive it; that we move in the direction that it seeks to move us, the direction of fuller communion with itself and with one another...I have very little of the mystic about me. I am such a hopelessly verbal person that even as I pray, I hear myself praying and worry about the words."

Buechner's conclusion at the end, that he has very little of the mystic in him because of his wordiness, even in prayer, is not inconsistent with his claim at the outset that "Every man is a mystic." For he did not say every man (or woman as I'm sure he would now add) is a mystic, period, regardless how he thinks or behaves. We are all mystics, rather, "because every man at one time or another experiences in the thick of his joy or his pain the power out of the depths of his life to bless him." I think Buechner is inviting us here to remember back to those intense times in our lives when we have been "in the thick of our joy or our pain." At such times he claims that we have each experienced an extraordinary thing: a power out of the depths of our life that has blessed us. What name, if any, that we might give to this power is not what matters to him. What "does matter, vastly, is that we open ourselves to receive it; that we move in the direction that it seeks to move us, the direction of fuller communion with itself and with one another." Mysticism, he seems to be saying, is movement rather than stasis, a progressive opening up to be led, a continual movement towards what he claims we are being led to: further communion. T. S. Eliot's *Four Quartets* comes to mind: "We must be still and still moving / Into another intensity / For a further union, a deeper communion..." Like I said, a lot to unpack, but profoundly worth the unpacking.

May Sarton

When the poet/novelist May Sarton brings mysticism to bear on ordinary tasks--cleaning and tidying are about as ordinary as you can get--she is making a profound point.

"There is a mystical rite under the material act of cleaning and tidying, for what is done with love is always more than itself." What Sarton is not saying here is that cleaning and tidying, in and of themselves, have anything necessarily to do with the mystical. But if they are done with love, that very investment of love turns them into a mystical rite. The connection here is unmistakable: mysticism has everything to do with love. You may think you haven't a mystical bone in your body, so to speak, but if you pour yourself lovingly into the task at hand, whatever that task may be, be filled with wonder to ponder May Sarton's pronouncement that indeed you are engaging in a mystical rite. Your love makes it so. And you thought priesthood or guruhood was a million miles removed.

I trust May would smile to assure Frederick Buechner that all those words in his prayers, springing from love, would not be one whit less a mystical rite.

Henry David Thoreau

"My desire for knowledge is intermittent; but my desire to commune with the spirit of the universe... is perennial and constant...The fact is I am a mystic, a transcendentalist, and a natural philosopher to boot."

The fact that Thoreau considered himself a transcendentalist as well as a natural philosopher does not comes as a surprise to any who have read him or know of his life. That the first designation he gives himself is "a mystic," however, gives a jolt. Thoreau the non-churchgoing one a mystic? Surely not, at least not according to the common view that mysticism refers to some lofty state or esoteric practice.

I can imagine Thoreau's ironic smile. What is *not* mystical about a desire to commune with the spirit of the universe? And if this desire is not intermittent, as is his intellect's desire for knowledge, but "perennial and constant," then we might allow this writer usually adept in his choice of words to use the best word he could think of to capture the essence of who he believes himself to be. I can't believe Henry David would want us to quibble over the word that he chose. What I think he *would* want us to do is to experience something of the joy that *he* experienced in his incessant desire to commune with the spirit of the universe.

James Michener

Immersed in Catholic Spain while he was writing *Iberia,* James Michener could not overlook the significance of the life and writings of St. Theresa of Avila for Spain in particular but more broadly for the Catholic Church.

"'A castle made of diamonds...a paradise in which God takes delight'--It is obvious that to an organized church the mysticism expressed here by Teresa poses a threat for it runs the risk of degenerating into the Quaker heresy of 'each man his own priest,' because if by the mystical process one can attain direct contact with God, the intercession of church and prelate is no longer essential."

In response to Theresa's mystical descriptions of the inner castle of her soul, Michener is reflecting here on the danger such mystics pose to the Church. In so doing, he highlights an essential feature of mystical experience--the fact that it is personal and immediate, meaning not mediated by an external authority. The experience itself is the authority! Growing up a Quaker, Michener understood well the threat posed to the Church by the Quaker conviction that there is "that of God" in absolutely every person, no exception. Where is the need of a priesthood if you can have that? Heresy! shout True Believers.

John Shelby Spong

Retired Episcopal Bishop of Newark John Shelby Spong had quite a lot to say about mysticism, starting with his claim that Jesus was a Jewish mystic whose intention was not to start a new religion but to purify his own religion. On social as well as theological grounds, Spong ruffled many feathers, much, he reminded us, as did Jesus.

Let's look to what Spong says about the Gospel of John. Those of fundamentalist or literalist inclination will find the going difficult if not infuriating here, but he did not write for these. In fact he *warns* of these. "John's Gospel is so profound, so poetic, so skillfully crafted, so dependent on images and concepts out of the Jewish past that it is worthy of the study of a lifetime that so many biblical scholars have given it. But it is distorted, trivialized, and made almost contemptible by those who cannot escape their commitment to the shallowness of only literal truth." Is there any wonder that Jack Spong is anathema to those of a literalist bent? How should John be read if not through a literalist lens, and what difference would it make? "When John's Gospel is read through the eyes of the mystic, it becomes a powerful narrative about the divine potential that is in all of life."

It likely will come as a shock to learn what did it for Spong, what needed to happen before the mystical insight took hold in him. "The death of the theistic definition of God has been for me the doorway into the mystical reality of the God who is beyond any definition." It is not the place here to try to dissect this bold statement, that it is precisely the theistic belief in a Creator separate from His/Her creation that he finally broke free from, that he feels Christians need to break free from if their religion is not to wither and die.

And where has his deepening of the place of the mystical led him with regard to Jesus? "A redefined Jesus still stands at the center of my God experience. He is not the one sent to be my savior, redeemer or rescuer...He is rather a God presence through whom I am empowered to be open to the life, love and being that flows through me. I now call myself a mystic because in my understanding of God I have gone beyond words into a kind of wordless wonder, awe and mystery. This is not where I was a decade ago. I doubt if it will be where I am a decade from now." Thus speaks a man for whom God has become verb instead of noun.

Ken Wilber

Ken Wilber, a modern philosopher of the spirit-mind, perhaps gets to the nub of this mysticism business with the following: " The aim of mystics is to deliver men and women from their battles by delivering them from their boundaries." How provocative to think of deliverance instead of salvation, and then to wonder what battles we might be freed from if our self-definition did not exclude others, the world, even God, if the true self that we are were indeed boundaryless? Wilber goes on: "A mystic is not one who sees God as an object [Spong's theistic God], but one who is immersed in God as an atmosphere." Follow the invitation here to our imagination: What difference would it make in my life if I kept coming back to the awesome realization that I, and every other separate-seeming person or thing in the universe, is immersed in God?

Wilber does not shy away from religious language, just sees it as metaphoric rather than literal: "The Christ figure is, to a mystic, a perfect embodiment and symbol of one's timeless and selfless Essence...Christ's revelation was an evolutionary advance of the Dharmakaya. 'I and the Father are one.'" Is what Christians term the Father manifested but once, twenty centuries ago in Palestine, or endlessly? Wilber makes clear which way he thinks mystics lean.

Gilbert Keith Chesterton

I count it a great blessing that my early adult life was immersed in the reading of Gilbert Keith Chesterton. The emphasis Chesterton placed on the supreme importance of taking with gratitude instead of for granted has remained a mainstay of my life's spirit journey. A convert from Anglicanism to Catholicism, he was not one to speak often of mysticism, but his philosophy of life was, to my way of thinking, mystical to the core. He hints at it in the following.

"I am interested in wooden posts which do startle me like miracles. To me the post is wonderful because it is there." He refers to this as his "original and almost mystic conviction of the miracle of all existence and the essential excitement of all experience...Most probably we are in Eden still. It is only our eyes that have changed." Ah, that kingdom again, at hand.

Further flowerings from the mystic-at-heart Chesterton: "At the back of our brains, so to speak, there was a forgotten blaze or burst of astonishment at our own existence. The object of the artistic and spiritual life was to dig for this submerged sunrise of wonder, so that a man sitting in a chair might suddenly understand that he is actually alive, and be happy."

And GKC once again: " The world will never starve for want of wonders, but only for want of wonder...The object of my school is to show how many extraordinary things even a lazy and ordinary man may see if he can spur himself to the singular activity of seeing...I will sit still and let the marvels and adventures settle on me like flies." Shades of Rumi 13 centuries earlier: "Mystics are experts in laziness. They rely on it, because they continuously see God working all around them. The harvest keeps coming in, yet they never even did the plowing." Wonder and gratitude, for both Chesterton and Rumi, are the bedrock.

Joseph Campbell

What Chesterton was for me in the 60s, the world mythologist Joseph Campbell was for me through the 70s and 80s. Electrifying is not too strong a word to capture the effect his writings had on me during those pivotal decades. The following highlights some of what drew me to him.

Regarding mysticism, Campbell gets to the heart of it: "Yielding to a larger opening—that's what mysticism is...The ego that relates to the other as to a 'Thou' is different from the ego that's relating to an 'It.' You can turn anything into a Thou. That's what the mystical experience is supposed to be."

When spelling out the vivifying nature of the myths of the world (myth meaning story, not falsehood), Campbell felt there was no better place to begin than with the mystical: "The first function of mythology is what I have called the mystical function: to waken and maintain in the individual a sense of awe and gratitude in relation to the mystery dimension of the universe, not so that he lives in fear of it, but so that he recognizes that he participates in it, since the mystery of being is the mystery of his own deep being as well."

Though moving beyond institutional religion, Campbell continued to mine the rich treasury of its imagery and symbols: "The mystical approach, what might be called the Pentecostal point of view: through your own inward experience, the divine mystery is revealed."

Finally, in our perilous time when we are witnessing a fierce resurgence of belligerent nationalism breeding not only xenophobia but disdain of Earth stewardship, we would do well to remember these words from Joseph Campbell: "This Earth, the one oasis in all space, an extraordinary kind of sacred grove, as it were, set apart for the rituals of life; and not simply one part or section of this Earth, but the entire globe now a sanctuary." Think if the flag to which the citizens of the world pledged their deepest allegiance, above even that of their nation, were the flag of the Earth! Now there's a vision that can save us.

Finally, listen to the premium Campbell places on the importance of having a sacred space: "To have a sacred space is an absolute necessity for anybody today...This is a place where you can simply experience and bring forth what you are and what you might be. This is the place of creative incubation." Sacred grove, sanctuary, sacred space, creative incubation--clearly a mystic is speaking here.

John Yungblut

After twenty years an Episcopal priest, John Yungblut became a Quaker in 1960. In his extensive writings over the next 35 years, mysticism became a recurring theme as it was primarily what had drawn him to Quakerism. "Quakers believe passionately in the continuing possibility of fresh revelation...They have determined to explore the potential of group mysticism, both an end in itself as well as an ethical mysticism—translating the love of God into the action of testimonies before the world."

It was not only this that caught my attention as I was myself gravitating toward the Quakers in the late 1980s. In addition it was Yungblut's embrace of other writers who also had become central to my vision of things. Having been influenced profoundly since my Jesuit days by Teilhard de Chardin, I was thrilled to discover Yungblut's own deep love of Teilhard who sang of "the diaphany of the divine at the heart of the universe on fire." And then it was Yungblut's reverence before titans in my own spirit journey, such as Thomas Merton and Joseph Campbell, and then these too: "Thomas Berry and Loren Eiseley—great mentors in leading the way to an Earth mysticism." Drawn for decades to the Earth mysticism of Native Americans, I could only cheer.

But it was Yungblut's placement of mysticism within both a depth psychological perspective on the one hand and an evolutionary perspective on the other that particularly spoke to me. Regarding the former, he often turned to another who had deeply impacted me, Carl Jung: "Individuation...the Quest of the Holy Grail. No enterprise could be fraught with more high adventure nor be more profoundly religious...Jung asserts that the archetypes of the self and the Self are ultimately indistinguishable. No mystic ever made a bolder claim!"

As regards the evolutionary: "Mystical consciousness is that human faculty, new in evolutionary perspective, in which we can actually perceive the as yet unfinished creation still at work. Just as life emerged from matter, thought from life, and spirit from thought, so mystical awareness now emerges from spirit." Incessantly Yungblut would come back to it, the relevance and the hope and the power and the beauty of this mystical vision. "Learn from the mystics how to be truly at home in the universe...The Earth, the very cosmos, is awaiting the development of more contemplatives who have become capable of mystical communion with the Earth...All you have to do is hear the heart of the Earth beating within you."

Perhaps John Yungblut's most insistent theme: "All are special kinds of mystics, at least potentially." So how are we to go about discovering our own inner mystic? He gives us a tantalizing hint: "Mystical religion is largely caught." What this says to me is that when I am in the presence of those who are *heart and soul alive*--I can see it in their eyes, hear it in their voice, feel it in their kindness toward themselves and the world--*something comes alive in me.* I catch a little of what they've got, then hope to spread the contagion.

Rufus Jones

John Yungblut had been deeply influenced by Rufus Jones, a Quaker whose impact on American Quakerism in the early 20th century was profound. A recurring theme for Jones was the relevance of mysticism, "the heart and core of all true religion." From the following, it seems clear that he would agree with Yungblut that mystical religion is largely caught.

"Mystical experience is much more common than is usually supposed...A great many persons never grasp and understand the inner flashes and intimations until some human helper brings a living personal interpretation which gives a sudden meaning to what was happening within...One leaps to his full height when the right inner spring is reached." Jones then recounted an experience in adolescence that changed his life. "You listen to a hundred persons unmoved and unchanged. You hear a few quiet words from the man with the kindling torch and you suddenly discover what life means." May each reader remember with gratitude an encounter of such kindling.

Jones continued in the same vein, extending the image of the kindling torch both to evolution and to Jesus: "In Jesus we have a master manifestation of that creative upward tendency of life, a surprising mutation...He is not a visitant or a stranger here in the world...It is only through a concrete person that we can be assured of love at the heart of things." A new way to think of Jesus: a master manifestation, a surprising mutation rising from Earth proclaiming love at the heart of things.

The very word prayer, dull from overuse, springs into life again when a mystic worthy of the name opens the bud of it to the sun: "Prayer is as natural as breathing," Jones assures us. "It is as normal as appreciation of beauty, or the pursuit of truth. The soul is made that way, and as long as men are made with mystical deeps within, they will pray and be refreshed. In those high-tide occasions when many human hearts together are fused in silent communion, tides from beyond our own margins sweep into us and refresh us...What we pray for affects the heart of God." There is much to ponder deeply here. To think--each one of us, through our own manner of prayer, can affect the heart of God!

A final reassurance from Rufus Jones: "Something large and luminous backs our deeds. When we are on right lines of advance, doors open before us...The conviction of presence enables the beholder to [with]stand the universe." Conviction of presence--perhaps no phrase better captures what is truest to the mystic.

Alan Watts

Alan Watts' many books sustained me back in the 1970s. Unabashed sensualist and mystic (seeing no contradiction between the two), he risked ruffling ecclesiastical feathers by importing riches from the East about the Divine found within. "My basic intuition: that here and now, without any artificial striving and straining, the flow of life in man is inseparably one with the Tao, the flow of the universe—call it God, Braham, the Divine Ground..." He goes on to clarify: "The God who made the world stands outside it as the carpenter stands outside his artifacts, but the Tao which grows the world is within it...God is the deepest inside of everything...The word 'God' is more of an exclamation than a proper name. It expresses astonishment, reverence, and even love for our reality."

Watts kept coming back to this basic theme: "The mystery of being is my supreme fascination, though, as a shameless mystic, I am more interested in religion as feeling and experience than as conception and theory." And he went on, "The truth that religion, to be of any use, must be mystical has always been denied by the seemingly large number of people, including theologians, who do not know what mysticism is...Its essence is the consciousness of union with God." Let's just say he had a beef with conventional theology.

And conventional theology had a beef with Alan Watts. How could it not when he would say things like this: "The only real atom—as Chardin put it—is the universe...Outwardly I am one apple among many. Inwardly I am the tree...This, then, is the taboo of taboos: you're IT!" Blasphemy indeed to the orthodox.

And then, dangerous message to the youth of the 60s, there was this business about psychedelics. "Psychedelic experience is only a glimpse of genuine mystical insight, but a glimpse which can be matured and deepened by the various ways of meditation in which drugs are no longer necessary or useful. When you get the message, hang up the phone." Drugs might open the door, even give a taste, but then the real work was to begin.

In a day when materialism was decried as the antithesis of the spiritual, Watts begged to differ, using cooking to make his point. "Proper cooking can be done only in the spirit of a sacrament and a ritual. It is an act of worship and thanksgiving, a celebration of the glory of life...Ritual: anything done with loving awareness and reverence [I can hear May Sarton cheering]...It is impossible to be a true materialist without being a mystic as well." Those fortified against hedonism had a formidable foe in Alan Watts.

Though we don't think of Watts as a poet, he had the makings: "The individual is so interwoven with the universe that he and it are one body....Man meets the world outside with a soft skin, with a delicate eyeball and eardrum, and finds communion with it through a warm, melting, vaguely defined, and caressing touch whereby the world is not set at a distance like an enemy to be shot, but embraced to become one flesh, like a beloved wife." Sensualist and mystic here join.

Not limiting his criticism to clerics, Watts included psychotherapists: "By and large, psychotherapists lacked the metaphysical dimension...They affected the mentality of insurance clerks and lived in a world scrubbed and disinfected of all mystery, magic, color, music and awe, with no place in the heart for the sound of a distant gong in a high and hidden valley." Does he not, without using the word mystical here, in touching upon mystery, magic, color, music and awe, evoke its essence?

Discovering years later the poet-mystic Hafiz, I can't but believe that he and Watts are frolicking somewhere in their shared whimsicality. I end with a favorite from whimsical Alan: "I did not alight in this universe like a bird arriving upon a branch from some alien limbo. I grew upon that branch like a leaf. For I am something which everything is doing; I am the whole process waving a flag named me, and calling out, 'Yoo-hoo!'" Next birthday, get out your flag and start waving, "Yoo hoo, here I am, what unique-in-all-the-universe gift!"

.

Thomas Berry

Building on Teilhard's great vision of a universe still birthing. Thomas Berry, cultural historian and prophet of Earth, had extraordinary things to say about the human capacity for the mystical.

"The archetypal journey of the universe can now be experienced as the journey of each individual. We are ourselves a mystical quality of the Earth, the garden planet of the universe... The human is the understanding heart of the universe."

Whoa now. A mystical quality of the Earth? The understanding heart of the universe? Wild hyperbole it would seem, poetic flight beyond poetic flights, but what if it were true?

Berry would have us believe it is and calls our attention to the inhabitants on this continent before the arrival of Columbus: "The European cultures have been especially limited in their ability to see the profoundly religious and spiritual qualities of the Indian traditions offering to the Euroamerican a mystical sense of the place of the human and other living beings, this art of communion."

Back we come to this sense of *communion* at the heart of the mystic's experience. But when it comes to the Earth, Berry laments a great estrangement: "In relation to the Earth, we have been autistic for centuries...We no longer hear the voice of the rivers, the mountains, the sea. The trees and meadows are no longer intimate modes of spirit presence. The world about us has become an 'it' rather than a 'thou'...We have lost our sense of courtesy toward the Earth."

As to how we might regain a sense of courtesy toward the Earth, he suggests we might begin by opening our eyes to daily miracles: "Dawn and sunset are the mystical moments in the diurnal cycle, the moments when the numinous dimension of the universe reveals itself with special intimacy...Do you simply see the sun rising or do you see the flaming forth of the deep mystery of the universe?" Back we are brought to the kingdom at hand, if only we waken to it.

Jack Good

As rich as was the reading of Jack Good's four books, even richer was the gift of his friendship. A member of the Roanoke Quaker community in his later years, Jack embodied the wisdom contained in his sermons and writings. Here is a sampling that relates to the mystical.

"One sad fact of our time is that the name of Rufus Jones is receding from religious memory. Jones was a Quaker and a mystic. His clear and persuasive writings influenced a generation of church leaders. The term 'mystic' means he was convinced of the nearness of the Divine." Convinced of the nearness of the Divine--a helpful phrase for any searching the meaning of mystic.

Another is the personal encounter with the Sacred: "Mystics, including modern Quakers, achieve similar spiritual results through their emphasis on that of God within both themselves and all other members of the human community. The mystical experience—the personal encounter with the Sacred—becomes sacramental. Every encounter with another human being is a moment of transcendence." Let these words sink in. Every encounter with another human being is, or can become, sacramental. Are we not back to the kingdom at hand?

And where does Good see Jesus fitting in? "Jesus was an incarnation of the Divine, but he was not unique in that role. The testimony of our biblical tradition is that every human being can be such an incarnation...Jesus never requested 'Worship me.' His challenge was 'Follow me.'...Jesus, as presented in the scriptures, was a man of action, not a weaver of dogmatic patterns. He practiced a reckless inclusiveness...a radical openness thereby destroying walls that had separated people. He gathered his closest friends from the edges of the social world." We might, in our search to reclaim the mystical, add reckless inclusiveness and radical openness.

Jack Good here introduces us to a new name for Spirit, more than personal, to be sure, but never less than personal: "An omnipotent God is being exchanged for an empowering God. A small, manageable deity is giving way to something like what I have called the Numen—the redemptive Spirit...By interacting with the created world, God continues to change just as the universe continues to change. God, too, is in process...The idea of a personal God is deeply embedded in our tradition for good reason. The Numen is much more than personal. But the Numen is never less than personal."

We might add another quality of mystics: ever on the lookout for new metaphors for the ineffable.

Loren Eiseley

Loren Eiseley mused upon the many labels that others had in the course of his life pinned on him, mystic among them. While he allowed there is likely a touch of truth in each, he suggested what we call him may have more to say about ourselves. "Some have called me Gothic in my tastes. Others have chosen to regard me as a Platonist, a mystic, a concealed Christian, a midnight optimist. Like most poets I am probably all these things by turns, or such speculations are read into me by those who are pursuing some night path of their own."

Here are some things from Eiseley's essays that incline me to believe he belongs in this present volume that is exploring the nuances and relevance of the mystical. It may be helpful to pause after each of these statements, letting the words penetrate.

"For many of us the biblical bush still burns, and there is a deep mystery in the heart of a simple seed."

And then this lovely conjecture about what makes sapphires in the dark: "Sometimes the rare, the beautiful, can only emerge or survive in isolation. In a similar manner, some degree of withdrawal serves to nurture man’s creative powers. There is love in atoms that makes sapphires in the dark." What a consciousness that discerns love in atoms!

Few things Eiseley wrote speak to me more deeply than this: “'Love not the world,' the biblical injunction runs...But I *do* love the world. I love its small ones, the things beaten in the strangling surf, the bird, singing, which flies and falls and is not seen again...I love the lost ones, the failures of the world."

And then the following from this ostensibly nonreligious man: "The story of the great saviors, whether Chinese, Indian, Greek, or Judaic, is the story of man in the process of enlightening himself through the slow inward growth of the mind...Ironically I who profess no religion find the whole of my life a religious pilgrimage...The acceptance of the supernatural is a widening of our grasp of the universe, its own numinous quality..." A new manner of conjecture on the supernatural is always welcome.

Could any book-lover not glory over this reimagining a library? "I walked down an echoing corridor through the long silent tiers of stacks that contained all the madness, all the wisdom, all the loneliness of centuries. Here imperishable thought lay waiting in the great social brain, waiting to strike fire in minds of similar affinities...Books, like ships, pass through seas of time and touch other minds in distant ages." Imperishable thought waiting to strike fire, books like ships sailing through seas of time--how are libraries not among humanity's shrines?

"Beyond lies the great darkness of the ultimate dreamer, who dreamed the light and the galaxies. Before act was, imagination grew in the dark. Man partakes of that ultimate wonder and creativeness." Simple words but electrifying meaning: Before act was, imagination grew in the dark! Take a week to ponder that one.

And then this from Eiseley to stretch our understanding of the miraculous: "We forget that nature itself is one vast miracle transcending the reality of night and nothingness. We forget that each one of us in his personal life repeats that miracle...We are in a creative universe. Let us then create." Could anything more ennoble the individual human being than the recognition not only of kinship but of identity with the vast miracle of a cosmos in the process of transcendence?

And finally, back to this mystic business: "I have had the experience of being labeled by that vague word 'mystic,' because I have not been able to shut out wonder occasionally, when I have looked at the world." Recognize the mystic in yourself if you, too, are unable to shut out this shout out from the soul we call wonder.

Richard Rohr

In recent years I've begun the day reading a reflection from Richard Rohr, Franciscan to his core, returning often to the mystical theme. "The words 'mystery,' 'mystical,' and 'mutter' all come from the Indo-European root word *muein,* which means to 'hush or close the lips.' We must start with humble, patient, wordless unknowing, sincere curiosity, or what many call 'beginner's mind.' Only then are we truly teachable. Otherwise, we only hear whatever confirms our present understanding." Ah, a question for us all to ponder: How truly are we teachable?

Here Rohr names a few who *were* truly teachable, able to see what was right in front of them. "A mystic—like Merton, Francis of Assisi, Julian of Norwich, John Duns Scotus, and many others—is one who recognizes God's image and likeness in *this* human being, in *this* creature, in *this* moment, and from that encounter with the sacred comes to see God everywhere and always. The mystic cannot help but love and have compassion for what is right in front of them. God's indwelling presence—in every created thing—is inherent and cannot be earned or destroyed." Duns Scotus, with his emphasis on the resplendent "thisness" of every existing thing, along with Gerard Manley Hopkins whose love-cry placed in the mouth of each mortal thing was "What I do is me, for that I came," have to be cheering from the wings.

Next Rohr hews to the essence: "Years ago, someone asked if I could sum up all my teachings in two words. My response was 'incarnational mysticism.' The first word, 'incarnational,' is Christianity's specialty and should always be our essential theme. We believe God became embodied."

Rohr goes on to acknowledge the difficulty many have with that second word. "Many Christians are scared of the word 'mysticism.' But a mystic is simply one who has moved from mere belief or belonging systems to actual inner experience of God." And then his interesting conjecture on why the Gospel of John does not speak to many: " So many readers are not moved by or attracted to John's Gospel because they were never taught the mystical mind."

Here is Rohr's understanding that the last place one with a mystical mind sits is high on a pedestal looking down on the unenlightened. "What mystics finally do, it seems to me, is heal in themselves the fragmentation that is evident in the world. Instead of hating, excluding, or dismissing it over there in others, they heal it in themselves. This healing is God's Spirit working in us. Mystics see the whole—good, bad, ugly, and beautiful—in themselves and others, refusing to hate or ignore any of it. This allows them to have immense sympathy, empathy, and compassion, and to work in service of the world's healing. " We can never adequately define the mystical, but what we *can* do is recognize its fruits: immense sympathy, empathy, compassion, and healing service.

Elsewhere Richard Rohr highlights another of mysticism's fruits , perhaps the most fundamental: overwhelming thanksgiving. "Religion's primary task is to lead people to say Thank You for the gift of life. It is to invite one into the 'cave of the heart' and to come face to face with a yearning to live and to be grateful for the gift of life, the gift of the universe and its 13.8 billion years of existence that have brought forth each of us and our species as a whole. Such a Thank You is mysticism, an overflow of the heart for our existence. This is why a great mystic like Meister Eckhart can say, "If the only prayer you say in your entire life is 'Thank You,' that would suffice."

Mirabai Starr

I have Richard Rohr to thank for this quotation from Mirabai Starr's *Wild Mercy: Living the Fierce and Tender Wisdom of the Women Mystics.* The connection she see between creativity and mysticism is profound, and her manner of expressing it resembles poetry more than prose. I will break up her long paragraph to better let the words sink in.

"There is a vital connection between creativity and mysticism. To engage with the creative impulse is to agree to take a voyage into the heart of the Mystery. Creativity bypasses the discursive mind and delivers us to the source of our being. When we allow ourselves to be a conduit for creative energy, we experience direct apprehension of that energy. We become a channel for grace.

"To make art is to make love with the sacred. It is a naked encounter, authentic and risky, vulnerable and erotically charged. The muse rarely behaves the way we would like her to, and yet every artist knows she cannot be controlled.

"Artistic self-expression necessitates periods of quietude in which it appears that nothing is happening. Like a tree in winter whose roots are doing important work deep inside the dark earth, the creative process needs fallow time. We have to incubate inspiration. We need empty spaces for musing and preparing, experimenting and reflecting.

"Society does not value its artists, partly because of the apparent lack of productivity that comes with the creative life. This societal emphasis on goods and services is an artifact of the male drive to erect and protect, to engineer and execute, to produce and control.

"Art begins with receptivity. Every artist, in a way, is feminine, just as every artist is a mystic. And a political creature. Making art can be a subversive act, an act of resistance against the deadening lure of consumption, an act of unbridled peacemaking disguised as a poem or a song or an abstract rendering of an aspen leaf swirling in a stream."

So what qualifies for being a mystic according to Mirabai Starr? Any who allow themselves to be a conduit for creative energy, thus agreeing to take a voyage into the heart of the Mystery.

Thomas Merton

Thomas Merton's regret over having few if any "mystical experiences" compared with many that he admired and wrote about is instructive. First, it is something that many of us can relate to, and is perhaps why we are reluctant to recognize that we, too, could be mystics. If no dazzling "sound and light show," then no mystic, right? Wrong, according to the multiple witnesses to the mystical we have been considering. Extraordinary auditory or visual experiences are not what it's about. These are gifts, not without danger of inflation, but they are not required. What is required, as we just saw with Richard Rohr, are things like sympathy, empathy, compassion, healing service. Listen to Thomas Merton to see if he qualifies.

"To be a member of the human race...like news that one holds the winning ticket in a cosmic sweepstake...There is no way of telling people that they are all walking around shining like the sun." This was Merton, sounding very much like a mystic, reflecting on his astonishment at the people passing by on a busy street corner one day in downtown Louisville.

Or this from Merton on the dawning of a new day: "The most wonderful moment of the day, the virgin point between darkness and light, is that when creation in its innocence asks permission to 'be' once again...The great presence of the sun...There are drops of dew that show like sapphires in the grass as soon as the morning sun appears...This presence and communion, the coming into being in the act of praise, is the heart of Old Testament worship as it is also of monastic choral praise."

Or this in praise of poets, sounding like one: "The solidarity of poets is an elemental fact like sunlight, like the seasons, like the rain...To read such poems is to live and move in splendor. Your heart becomes a tropical palace, opening out on the seven seas, and all the continents with spice ships coming to you from everywhere, and the soft voices of the Antilles speaking from the heart of the sun." Poet, mystic, sometimes it's hard to tell. And sometimes it's hard not to be reminded of a wandering Jew in Galilee long ago. "I feel fire and music in the Earth under my feet...By ceasing to question the sun I have become light, bird and wind...My leaves sing. I am Earth..."

Consider that contemplative in the following is interchangeable with mystic: "The most dangerous man in the world is the contemplative, who is guided by nobody."

Here are Merton's reflections about another mystic: "Teilhard is a providential combination of the scientist and the mystic...He has hocked everything and bet it on the human species." May we borrow from them both their unflinching faith in the human species.

The following words of Thomas Merton, which I first read a full fifty years ago, come back to me each time I listen to the festival of the rain. Be careful what you read. It can leave a mark on you. "Rain is a festival...What a thing it is to sit absolutely alone, in the forest, at night, cherished by this wonderful, unintelligible, perfectly innocent speech, the most comforting speech in the world."

Extraordinary mystical experiences that take us out of ourselves are not what our search has been about. Listening with all our inner and outer senses to the present moment which we inhabit, which inhabits us, well, thanks to guides like Thomas Merton, maybe that catches it best. The kingdom is at hand.

Conclusion

So have we hit the mother lode in our search for the gold at the heart of the words mystical, mystic or mysticism? Likely not, but the wise members of our species we have been considering have left valuable clues into the mystical.

> **Albert Einstein**: the most beautiful emotion we can experience; the power of all true art and science; whenever we stand rapt in awe.
>
> **Karl Rahner**: the mark of the Christian of the future if Christianity is to survive; experiencing God for real.
>
> **Carl Rogers**: part of something larger; found in relationships of healing presence when spirits reach out to each other.
>
> **Jalal-al-Din Rumi**: submission; remembering; flying from moment to moment as the harvest keeps coming in.
>
> **Matthew Fox**: experiential union with creation and its unnamable mysteries; believing there is a conspiracy of the universe on our behalf; compatible with a warrior's thirst for justice (defending what one cherishes).
>
> **Frederick Buechner**: experiencing, in the thick of our joy and our pain, a power that blesses us; what doesn't matter, what we name it; what does matter, opening ourselves to receive it; the direction of fuller communion.

May Sarton: cleaning and tidying can be mystical rites; what is done with love is always more than itself.

Henry David Thoreau: desiring to commune with the spirit of the universe.

James Michener: direct contact with God makes intercession of church no longer essential.

John Shelby Spong: John's Gospel: metaphorical, not literal, narrative about divine potential in all of life; Jesus: a God presence through whom we are empowered; wordless wonder, awe and mystery.

Ken Wilber: delivers us from our battles by delivering us from our boundaries; immersed in God as an atmosphere.

Gilbert Keith Chesterton: startled by wooden posts--they are there!; most probably we are in Eden still; it's enough to sit in a chair and be happy; gratitude and wonder.

Joseph Campbell: yields to a larger opening; can turn any It into a Thou; wakens and maintains awe and gratitude towards the mystery dimension of the universe; the Pentecostal point of view--through your own inward experience, the divine mystery is revealed; the entire globe: a sanctuary.

John Yungblut: the potential of group and ethical mysticism is what drew him to Quakers; the Earth mysticism of Native Americans can lead us home; truly at home in the universe; hear the heartbeat of Earth within you; all are mystics, at least potentially; less taught than caught.

Rufus Jones: the heart and soul of all true religion; much more common than is usually supposed; listening to one with the "kindling torch" makes all the difference; Jesus, a surprising mutation rising from Earth; something large and luminous backs our deeds; conviction of presence.

Alan Watts: the flow of each life is inseparable from the flow of the universe; God: the deepest inside of everything, more an exclamation than a proper name; outwardly I am one apple among many, inwardly I am the tree; when you get the message, hang up the phone (drugs); ritual: anything done with loving awareness and reverence; cooking: sacramental, a celebration of the glory of life; sensualist and mystic join; mystery, magic, color, music, awe. I am the whole process waving a flag named me, calling out "Yoo-hoo!"

Thomas Berry: we are ourselves a mystical quality of the universe; sense of communion, everything a Thou instead of an It; a sense of courtesy toward the Earth, with Native Americans our guides; dawn and sunset: mystical moments.

Jack Good: convinced of the nearness of the Divine; the personal encounter with the Sacred; Jesus: an Incarnation, not unique; reckless inclusiveness, radical openness; the Numen: more than personal but never less than personal.

Loren Eiseley: the biblical bush still burns; there is love in atoms that makes sapphires in the dark; I love the lost ones, the failures of the world; imperishable thought waiting to strike fire, books like ships sailing through seas of time; before act was, imagination grew in the dark; we are in a creative universe. Let us then create.

Richard Rohr: we are only truly teachable when we have a "beginner's mind"; incarnational mysticism: from mere belief to actual inner experience; permeates the Gospel of John; sees the whole--good, bad, ugly and beautiful--in themselves and others, refusing to hate or ignore any of it; religion's primary task: to lead people to say Thank You for the gift of life...Such a Thank You is mysticism, an overflow of the heart for our existence; immense sympathy, empathy, compassion, healing service.

Mirabai Starr: vital connection with creativity; conduits of creative energy, channels for grace; making art is making love with the sacred; needed for incubation: empty space.

Thomas Merton: everyone is walking around shining like the sun; presence and communion; poet, mystic, sometimes it's hard to tell; they are most dangerous who are guided by nobody; festival of rain: the most comforting speech in the world.

Charles C. Finn
January 2020

Appendix

Prose Yielding to Poetry.

Not Off in a Cave Somewhere

A mystic needn't be blinded by light,
visited by extraordinary powers,
off rapturous in a cave somewhere.
Not that there isn't light, power and rapture,
but it's likely the unspectacular sort
prompting attention to each new thing:
hello again, God,
how's it going, Tao?
The secret mystics and dancers share
isn't off in a cave somewhere.

Grailkingdom Come

You are a mystic
regardless whether you have a religion
if your spirit inclines you to open out,
your soul inclines you to bow down,
your heart inclines you to fold within.
Harvesting plenitude of past,
nurturing seed of future,
the diaphanous present grailkingdom's moment
holds all there is.

Belittled or Banned

Churches holding tight to their authority
fear mystics most of all.
The ultimate truth for the mystic
is that experienced within.
If Church or Book contradicts,
Church or Book is transcended--
anathema to True believers!
No wonder mystics down fearful ages
have been belittled or banned.

Mystic's Credo

"This is something I want to tell you very strongly.
Don't do anything...
The most powerful magic in the whole world
is working for us.
Relax and let it work."
The mystic's credo
is here captured by John Steinbeck
in a letter to his love.

What Helped Me Not Panic

What helped me not panic
when preparing to face fire from a dragon
was a line from a poem by Rumi
about my life not being my own.
I am not only lived by God
but propelled by ancestors within
and their thousand sustaining winds.
Ah, if we but remember who carries us,
whom we carry within.

Neither Color nor Creed Needed

Black Elk in his surface life
served as a Catholic catechist
for the Jesuits at Pine Ridge Reservation—
for decades their right hand native man.
Imagine their consternation
to discover in *Black Elk Speaks*
his unregenerate pagan soul.
Imagine, too, John Neihardt's awe
to be the one the old Indian chose
to entrust his great vision.
Mystics need neither color nor creed to bind them.

The Mystic's Advantage

Mystics have a distinct advantage.
Jesus' mandate to love others as self
has for centuries been a stumper—
lofty ideal, for sure, and nice poetry
but not within practical reach.
No other way would humans have made it so far,
goes the pragmatist's mantra,
than by dint of aggressive self-love.
Enlightened self-interest might well include
cooperation,
but if it ever comes down to other versus self,
smart money goes always on self.
Psych 101 here, whether grounded in Freud or
Skinner.
But mystics with deeper grounding
have come to experience a Self wider,
so when Jesus calls boldly for the seemingly naïve,
the hopelessly impractical,
when he talks about self and other being one in the
Father,
what others dismiss as theatrical or delusional
mystics accept as foundational.
When it comes to understanding Jesus,
mystics have the decided edge.

Risking All

Courage comes first to mind
when I think of Jack Spong.
Multiple death-threats notwithstanding,
he keeps on well into his eighties
daring to speak truth to the power
of fundamentalism's dying distortions of Jesus
in favor of a Jewish mystic's revelatory call
to awaken to our participation in the Great I Am.
Risking all to live fully,
love wastefully,
be all that he can be,
Spong invites those of every or no religion,
especially growing numbers of exiles *from* religion,
joyfully to discover religion's mystical heart,
then dare to come follow.

A Salute to Thomas Merton

The late 60s and early 70s—
these for me were the changing years.
You wouldn't expect a Trappist monk,
cloistered in the foothills of Kentucky,
to be the eloquent critic of racism and war
that raised my political consciousness,
but neither would you expect this same monk
to be the first to open my eyes
to the wisdom of nontheistic Zen.
His welcoming the wealth of the worlds of others
kept enriching his own.
What never wavered was his contemplative spirit
making his hermitage in the woods his keenest delight.
Words he wrote there about the festival of rain
have nourished me ever since
when rain comes with her blessing.
A salute to you, Tom Merton,
for daring to challenge hypocrisy in church and state,
for emboldening mystic kin across Earth,
for celebrating each morning's new miracle,
yes, and for taking up pen after listening to the rain
to call others to join in the festival.

A Few of the Ringing Reasons

Joseph Campbell's Catholic roots,
Celtic ancestry,
attraction to Native Americans,
debt to Krishnamurti,
affinity to Jung,
rapture before Chartres,
rejection of the literal for the metaphoric,
inclination towards the mystical
are but a few of the ringing reasons
my bond with him goes deep.

Reading Eiseley, Discovering Me

I wouldn't say Loren Eiseley instructs me
as much as confirms me,
shows me how vastly I cherish solitude,
prefer mystery,
value continuity,
bow in awe before time,
cheer evolution,
quest God,
love the living Earth.
Such pleasure to be following my bliss,
to be reading Eiseley and discovering me!

Mystical Accord

A languishing cat in my lap purring softly
enhances my dignity,
deepens my respect for trusted me.
Here is this animal sleek and lithe,
miniscule kin to the mighty lion,
less inclined to socializing than solitary pursuit--
here this furtive-by-nature cat
trusts me so much that his entire body
comforted by my presence
literally vibrates with contentment.
Purr doesn't do justice
to a testimonial to the benediction of affection,
to the mystical accord between sentient beings.
Ah, bound to my heart Dromia,
how your trust not only enamors me of you
but ennobles me!

An Inch Before Too Late

Gaia:
vital cell
within mystical body
of living cosmos
but increasingly imperiled
by plundering human unkind
at last thankfully awakening
(as divine drama would have it)
an inch before too late.

Spoken Like a Mystic

Paul Winter on his own music:
"The message is simply beauty, the beauty of sounds.
It's simply our celebration
of places and creatures that we love,
just as a typical pop song
is some man's celebration of the girl he loves.
It doesn't matter what you're loving."
Spoken like a mystic whose romance is inexhaustible
for being coextensive with the world.

The Only Wealth That Matters

The number of things that catch up your breath
marks the only wealth that matters.
Mystics across luminous Earth
receptive to the universal benediction
are stopped incessantly in their tracks,
hearts arrested by kindness and courage and beauty.
Inclined to awe and praise,
they shout magnificence to all who can hear.
Right now for me it's thunder and rain
in the wake of stupendous bright flashing!

Nourishment for Mystics

Catholics and Quakers,
for all their differences,
share a common affinity for communion—
for one, the culmination of their most sacred ritual,
for the other, the entire ritual.
Mystic sojourners can be nourished by either.

Wide Open

A mystic of any ilk
would have to get off on a motorcycle ride.
First there's the wind--
in a car you don't feel it unless the top's
    down,
but even then you're still snug inside.
On a bike you're wide open!
Even on a calm evening the wind met me,
enveloped me with such sustained rushing
that it would have been bliss sweet enough
just to sit back and *feel* it.
Add to that the connection to Earth--
you become one with her,
one with the pulsing road,
smells surrounding and penetrating
(o honeysuckle of early June!).
The view is more encompassing now,
both more comprehensive and more subjective
    now--
no more outer and inner you're in it!
Mystic or not, jump at the freewheeling chance if
    you get it
for an experience past exhilarating,
past the possibility of capture by mere words
of FREEDOM.

Enough to Give me Pause

If I have to keep breathing to keep existing,
then air must be part of my identity,
my "I am" must transcend my skin
to include the very atmosphere.
But then what about the sun I'm warmed by,
Earth that has given me birth,
plants and flesh I consume,
human beings without whose love I couldn't live?
Are not all integral to my being,
of necessity included when I say "I am"?
Maybe there's only one great I AM
the immortal divinity of which each mortal thing
incarnates.
It's enough to give me pause
when I pause to take a breath
and say "I am."

Training In Practical Mysticism

Contemplativa in actione--
rallying cry of Ignatius of Loyola
to his sons in the Company of Jesus.
The way Ignatius' vision had it,
action was not an alternative to contemplation
but its fruition!
For a training in practical mysticism,
one could do worse than spend ten growing years
with sons of Ignatius in the Company of Jesus.

No Derision There

It's tempting not to use "mystical"
for the obfuscation surrounding it,
for connotations ranging from derisive epithet to
 luminous vision.
But when groping to address the underlying great
 mystery,
when searching for a word to serve as a pointer,
mystical came closest.
That's my guess why Albert Einstein
wrote from an inspiration that the highest aspiration,
the deepest exploration,
carries us to the mystical.
When he reached for the richest word
to capture his awe before the universe,
mystical came closest.
No derision there.

Author's Biography

Born and bred in Cincinnati, Ohio, Charlie Finn's full embrace of Catholicism led him to enter the Society of Jesus (Jesuits) after high school. His ten years in the order, coinciding with the upheavals of the 60's (civil rights, Vatican II, Vietnam, multiple assassinations...), were transformative. After leaving the Jesuits in 1969, he lived for the next decade in Chicago where he switched careers from teaching to counseling and met and married Penny. After a year of traveling, the two of them settled in the mountains of southwest Virginia in 1979 where they have lived ever since on thirteen acres north of Roanoke. Two adopted children, April and Adam (now off on their own), along with multiple beloved animals and many flower and vegetable gardens have rounded out their rich life. Charlie has had a counseling practice in Roanoke, specializing in addictions, life transitions, and the spirit journey, until his retirement in September 2015. He now has even more time for travel, gardening, and, of course, writing.

Along the way writing became as important to him as counseling. Prior to the Jesuits he loved literature but never even considered writing until a young priest's passionate readings of the poetry of Gerard Manley Hopkins and Charles Peguy opened up for him the power and the beauty of the world of poetry. His own output of poetry then began but was miniscule up until the mid-80s, though his journaling in the years prior was extensive. In 1985, no doubt influenced by first child arriving and only sister dying, the creative floodgates opened. Poetry flowed from him over the ensuing years until enough had accumulated for him to begin to group his poems according to theme and to start publishing, then self-publishing, these collections. His works also include books of essays, church talks, historical works relating to America's Civil War, mandalas celebrating memory, and a Pendle Hill pamphlet. They can be ordered from him directly at *charles.c.finn@gmail.com or from his website at www.poetrybycharlescfinn.com*. They include the following:

Circle of Grace: In Praise of Months and Seasons (1995)
Natural Highs: An Invitation to Wonder (1999)
For the Mystically Inclined (2002)
Contemplatively Sweet: Slow-Down Poems to Ponder (2004)
Earthtalks: Conjectures on the Spirit Journey (2004)
The Elixir of Air: Unguessed Gifts of Addiction (2004)
Deep Joy, Steep Challenge: 365 Poems on Parenting (2005)
Earth Brother Jesus: Musings Free of Dogma (2005)
Embraced It Will Serve You: Encounters with Death (2006)
If a Child, Why Not a Cosmos? Lovesongs to Earth and Evolution (2006)
Fuel for War: Patriotic Entrancement (2006)
Earth Pleasures: Pets, Plants, Trees and Rain (2007)
Ithaca is the Journey: A Personal Odyssey (2007)
Steppingstones to the Civil War: Slavery Integral to Each (2008)
Aging Liberal Nostalgic for Vision (2008)
Empathy is the Key: Toward a Civil War Healing (2009)
Gentle Warrior John Yungblut: Guide on the Mystic's Journey (2009)
Full Heart Singing: Letters and Poems to a Girlchild (2009)
The Mastery of the Thing!: Transcendence in Counseling and Sports (2010)
Crafting Soul into Words: a Poet Sings of the Journey (2011)
Please Hear What I'm Not Saying: A Poem's Reach Around the World (2011)

Root and Wings: Gifts from Parents (2012)
*John Yungblut: Passing the Mystical Torch (*Pendle Hill Pamphlet #417, 2012)
Building a Memory Cathedral: Wisdom Figures .(2013)
O the Mind, Mind Has Mountains: Searching for the Heart of Hopkins (2015)
Building a Memory Cathedral: Years, Decades, Months (2015)
Mandalas Serving Memory: New Ways to Celebrate Your Life (2016)
New Under the Sun: Fecund 2016 (2017)
Focusing on Just One Gift: One Hundred Selected Poems (2018)
Great Day in the Morning: One Hundred Selected Poems (2019)
Sixty to Sing Of: A Wealth of Guardians (2019)
Winter Offerings: Poetry and Prose Dancing (2019)
Mining for Gold: Climbing Mount Empathy and Reclaiming the Mystical (2020)

Finn's spirit journey has been diverse and rich. Grounded in Catholicism, then seminary-steeped in it, he reached a point in the early 70s when its exclusive claims and dogmatic approach became too narrow for him and he parted ways not only from Catholicism but from institutional (versus mystical) Christianity. For the next fifteen years he considered himself a spiritual maverick letting his love of reading and travel open him up to the wealth of many paths. Influences particularly strong on him as he followed his bliss were Taoism, Native American spirituality, and the Creation-Centered spirituality of Matthew Fox and Thomas Berry. A special joy was to discover as he journeyed that, though leaving behind organized religion, his bond with Jesus only deepened.

“Ripeness is all,” as Shakespeare reminded us, and what Finn now realizes in retrospect is that he was ripening all along towards Quakerism which began insinuating into his life in the mid-to-late 80s. The bond with Jesus the mystic, the Jesuit focus on “contemplation in action” and “finding God in all things,” the Taoist trust in Way opening, Native American spirituality’s Earth mysticism, the Creation-Centered emphasis upon ongoing creation and revelation—all found for him sweet fruition in the simplicity and profundity of the Quaker way. A member of the Roanoke Monthly Meeting of the Religious Society of Friends, this spiritual maverick, even as he continues to journey, has found home.

www.ingramcontent.com/pod-product-compliance
Lightning Source LLC
LaVergne TN
LVHW050936080826
845145LV00004B/1281

* 9 7 8 1 7 9 4 8 9 1 5 8 6 *